/99

This book
belongs to

....

CD-ROM
FACT*finders*
INTERACTIVE MULTIMEDIA

ANCIENT TIMES

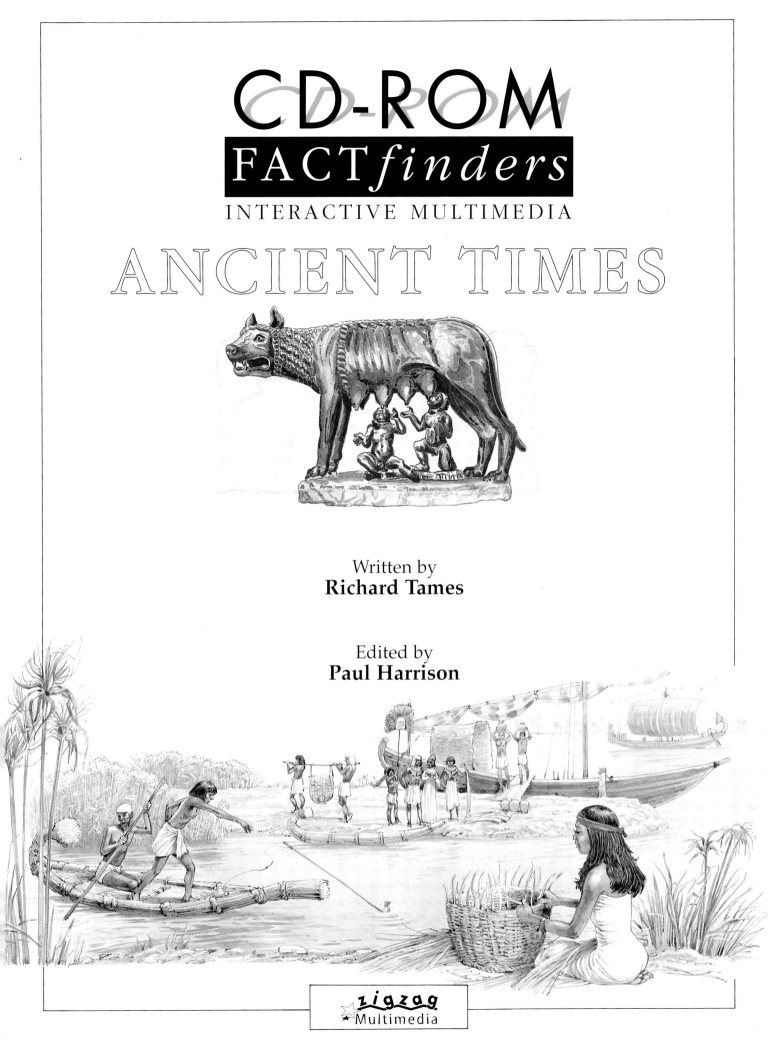

Written by
Richard Tames

Edited by
Paul Harrison

zigzag
Multimedia

The author, Richard Tames, has written over sixty books for children. He is also a qualified London 'Blue Badge' Guide.

ZIGZAG PUBLISHING

Published by Zigzag Publishing,
a division of Quadrillion Publishing Ltd.,
Godalming Business Centre, Woolsack Way,
Godalming, Surrey GU7 1XW, England.

Series concept: Tony Potter
Senior Editor: Nicola Wright
Design Manager: Kate Buxton
Production: Zoë Fawcett and Simon Eaton
Designed by: Maureen and Gordon Gray
and Kate Buxton
Illustrated by: Ed Org, Hemesh Alles,
Peter Dennis, Philip Hood and Steven Young
Cover design: Clare Harris

Colour separations: Scan Trans, Singapore
Printed in Singapore

Distributed in the U.S. by SMITHMARK PUBLISHERS
a division of U.S. Media Holdings, Inc.,
16 East 32nd Street, New York, NY 10016

Copyright © 1997 Zigzag Publishing. First published 1995.

ISBN 0-7651-9347-7
8411

Contents

About this book

This book tells you all about the earliest civilizations. The word civilization comes from a Latin word which means "living in cities".

The coming of civilization led to the invention of writing and wheeled transport, and advances in mathematics and medicine. It also meant the creation of large-scale armies and the growth of great empires by conquering other people's land. Although these early civilizations ended long ago, what they did still affects us today; and every year we discover more about what they were like.

This book will give you the answers to some of the most important questions you may ask about the past.

Where did civilization begin?

Under Babylonian law, a son who hit his father had his hands chopped off.

T he oldest known civilizations began in the area we now call the Middle East. Some cities, such as Damascus and Jericho, are at least 5,000 years old.

Q How big were the earliest cities?

A The earliest cities were nowhere near as large as modern cities. Çatal Hüyük, in what is now Turkey, was built about 9,000 years ago and had a population of only 5,000. The houses were made of mud bricks and were built up against each other, so there were no streets. People got in and out of their houses through holes in the roof using ladders.

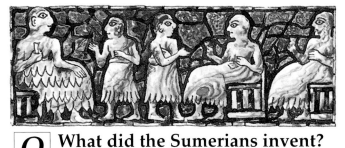

Q What did the Sumerians invent?

A The Sumerians knew how to weave cloth, make things out of metal and make pots on a wheel. But the most important progress they made was in writing, mathematics and astronomy. Their discoveries in these areas enabled them to keep records of taxes and agreements, write down laws and work out a calendar.

Q Where was Mesopotamia?

A Mesopotamia means "the land between the rivers." The area was in what is now Iraq. The rivers were the Tigris and the Euphrates, and the first city dwellers there were known as Sumerians. By 3000 B.C. there were powerful city states, such as Ur and Uruk, which traded with and fought against each other. The cities had populations of up to 50,000 people and were often built around mud-brick temples called ziggurats.

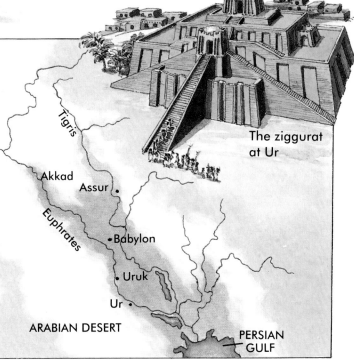

The ziggurat at Ur

Tigris

Akkad
Assur

Euphrates

Babylon

Uruk

Ur

ARABIAN DESERT

PERSIAN GULF

The oldest known set of false teeth belonged to a Phoenician man of 1000 B.C. He had four of someone else's teeth tied to his own with gold wire.

Sargon of Akkad

Q **Which were the most powerful city states?**

A Sargon of Akkad (2370 B.C.) was the first great conqueror that we know about. The Hittites created an empire based around Anatolia between 1800 B.C. and 1200 B.C. The Assyrians were a war-like people from the city state of Assur. They built a huge empire stretching from the Persian Gulf to Egypt, between 800 B.C. and 650 B.C.

Q **What was their writing like?**

A The first writing was pictographic. This means that instead of using letters and words, the Sumerians drew pictures. Later, these pictures came to represent sounds rather than actual objects. Sumerian writing is called "cuneiform," which means "wedge-shaped," because they used a sharp wedge to make marks in the clay tablets on which they wrote.

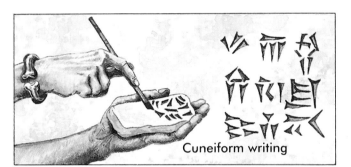

Cuneiform writing

Q **Where did civilization begin in in the Mediterranean?**

A The Minoan people began to build palaces on the island of Crete around 2200 B.C. The Palace of Knossos could hold up to 80,000 people. Around 1400 B.C. the Minoans were conquered by the Mycenaeans from mainland Greece.

Chess was invented in ancient India as a war game.

The Indus Valley stretches from Tibet, through Pakistan, to the Indian Ocean. The River Indus flows through this valley. Many ancient towns have been discovered there.

Q What was life like in the Indus Valley?

A Two major cities, called Mohenjo Daro and Harappa, have been found in this area, along with the sites of over one hundred other towns. From these ruins scientists have been able to discover many things about this ancient civilization. However, archaeologists have not been able to read the type of writing used by the Indus people at this time, so we still know very little about the way they lived.

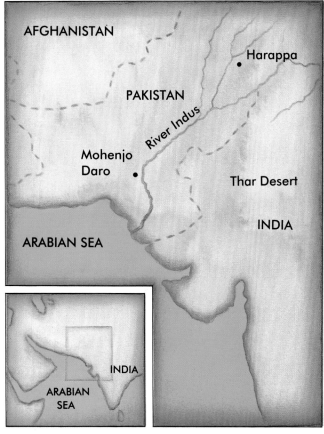

Q How long ago did these cities exist?

A They were probably built around 2500 B.C. and later abandoned around 1500 B.C. Each one was nearly 3 miles in circumference. No one is quite sure why these cities were abandoned, but the most likely explanation is that the Indus River changed course, moving away from the cities.

Q Why were cities built in this area?

A The people of the Indus Valley relied on the annual flooding of the river to provide the mineral-rich silt that made the farmland fertile. Owing to this, all the major towns and cities were built close to the river.

Merchants in Mohenjo Daro used to stamp their goods with seals. Nobody is sure if different merchants used different pictures on their seals, but there have been many different sorts found.

Q Was life in Mohenjo Daro well organized?

A The city was laid out on a rigid street plan and had the world's first known sewer system with drains and manholes. There were wide streets and large granaries for storing food in case the harvest failed. Houses were made out of bricks that were the same size, rather than oddly-shaped pieces of stone. Each house also had its own bathroom and toilet.

Q How did people dress?

A The Indus Valley people were the first in the world to grow cotton and make it into cloth. They also used copper to make jewelery. Men made razors out of copper.

Q What sort of transport did people use?

A Two-wheeled ox carts carried heavy loads over land, and boats were used to transport things up and down the river. Camels and pack horses were used to carry merchants' goods over long distances.

Q What did people do in their spare time?

A They kept pets such as dogs, cats, monkeys, caged birds and insects. Children played with whistles and toys, like pottery monkeys, which danced on pieces of string. Adults played dice games.

8

What is a dynasty?

荷葉飯

China has the oldest continuous civilization in the world. The country was ruled by different royal families known as dynasties. Little is known about the earliest part of Chinese history.

Q Where did civilization begin in China?

A The first powerful kingdom we know about was based near the fertile Yellow River around 1500 B.C. and was ruled by the Shang Dynasty. In 1027 B.C. the Shang were driven out by the Zhou, who ruled for 800 years.

Q What is the Great Wall of China?

A The Great Wall is the longest wall in the world. It is 2,150 miles long, stretching from the coast to the Gobi Desert. It was meant to keep out invaders from the north, but didn't always do so. The wall was built between 221 B.C. and 206 B.C., and strengthened by later emperors. Most of the present wall was rebuilt during the Ming Period (1368-1644).

Q Who was the first Emperor of the whole of China?

A In 221 B.C. the cruel and ruthless Qin ruler, Cheng, began to call himself Emperor of China. The Qin had overthrown the Zhou in 225 B.C. and ruled the biggest empire seen in history up to that time. Cheng also built the Great Wall of China.

9

Q Why was silk important?

A Silk was China's main export, sent right across Asia, and even as far as Rome, along trading routes that became known as the "Silk Route." The silk came from the cocoons of silkworms and made a light, soft, strong thread. The Chinese learned how to rear silkworms, feeding them on mulberry leaves. They kept the secret of how to make silk to themselves until 550 A.D., when two Persian monks smuggled silkworms out of China in a hollow cane.

Q What did the Chinese invent?

A The Chinese discovered many different things, including how to make paper and porcelain, a kind of fine pottery. They also discovered that the resin of the lacquer tree could be used to coat wooden bowls so they could hold hot foods and liquids, such as soup. Wheelbarrows were in use a thousand years before they became common in Europe.

Q Who was Confucius ?

A Confucius was a scholar whose ideas about government were influential in China, as well as in other countries. He thought that peace and order were the greatest blessings a country could have. He believed that a ruler should be just and kind and his subjects should be loyal and obedient. Confucius also taught the importance of good manners and self-control.

Q What advances did the Chinese make in science?

A Wang Chong, who lived in the first century A.D., showed that eclipses and the movements of the stars and the moon could be predicted. Zhang Heng made the world's first seismograph, used to detect and record earthquakes. The Chinese also invented a kind of medicine, called acupuncture, which cures people by sticking needles in them.

Pictured is a seismograph. Balls dropped into the frogs' mouths when an earthquake occurred. The more balls that fell, the stronger the earthquake.

The Olmecs carved large stone heads which were up to 8.8 feet high.

People migrated from Asia to the American mainland about 30,000 years ago. Sea levels were lower then, and North America was joined to Russia by a land bridge. The first advanced civilizations grew up in Central America.

Q Which were the first important civilizations that we know of?

A The Olmecs lived along the eastern coast of what is now Mexico. Their civilization flourished between 1150 B.C. and 800 B.C. Their sculptures and pottery influenced later cultures. The Maya, from what is now Guatemala, were also important. They flourished between 300 B.C. and 900 A.D.

Q How advanced were they?

A The people of Central America knew about farming, pottery and writing and how to make things out of gold, copper and jade. They also made paper from the bark of wild fig trees. However, they had no knowledge of such things as iron, glass, coins, or the plough.

Q What did the people of Central America eat?

A The basic diet was made up of maize, beans, tomatoes, chili peppers and turkeys. People also reared dogs and guinea pigs to eat.

Q What did they use instead of iron?

A For making weapons and cutting tools they used obsidian, a kind of volcanic glass. When it is polished, obsidian has a very sharp edge, though it does break easily.

The Mayas used melted rubber to make waterproof clothing.

Chocolate was first brought to Europe from Central America, where it was made with chilli peppers.

Q **Did they know about the wheel?**

A They knew about the wheel but only used it on toys and not for transport. This was probably because they had no animal strong enough to pull a cart.

Q **What was their religion like?**

A They worshipped gods who represented the Sun, Moon, rain and maize. Human sacrifice was common and caused many wars as city states wanted to capture prisoners to sacrifice.

Q **Did they play games?**

A We know that they played a game which involved hitting a hard rubber ball at stone markers along the sides of a walled court. Heads, elbows, knees and shoulders could be used to hit the ball, but you could not use hands or feet. During festivals games were played in honor of the gods, and the loser became a human sacrifice.

Q **Can any of the cities still be seen?**

A About forty cities have been discovered so far. The most important buildings were stepped pyramids, used for religious ceremonies. Teotihuacan (which means "Where Men become Gods"), near modern Mexico City, had a population of 200,000 and covered 7.7 sq. mi. The main street was 1.2 mi. long and 130 ft. wide, with over a hundred temples along its sides. The largest building, the Pyramid of the Sun, was over 230 feet high.

AFRICA
Tanzania

Were there cities in Africa?

The oldest human remains in the world have been found in Tanzania.

Ancient Africa's greatest civilization developed in Egypt. But there were other important states along its northern coast and in what are now the present-day countries of Sudan and Ethiopia.

Q Did people ever live in the Sahara?

A The Sahara has not always been a desert, and people used to live there until 2000 B.C. Historians know they herded cattle, made pottery, and used four-wheeled vehicles, either as war chariots or as carts for transport.

Q What happened after the Sahara had become a desert?

A The Sahara started to dry up around 10,000 B.C. Some people still managed to live in oases where there was enough water for date palms and their livestock. By using camels, which could go without water for days, traders were able to cross 186 miles of desert in a week. They bought salt and cloth from the north in exchange for slaves, gold and leather from the south.

Q What was Carthage?

A Carthage was originally a colony, founded near present-day Tunis, by the Phoenicians. They were a trading people who lived in what is now Lebanon. In their language it was called Kart-Hadasht, which means "New Town." Carthage grew rich and powerful through trade and its silver mines.

Q What happened to Carthage?

A The Romans feared the growing power of Carthage, and fought three great wars over a hundred years. The Romans were finally victorious in 146 B.C. They totally destroyed Carthage and ploughed up the land where it had once stood.

Q Which was the first great empire of eastern Africa?

A The kingdom of Kush, probably founded by people from Egypt, rose on the banks of the Nile River. The kings of Kush were buried in pyramids, like Egyptian pharaohs. The first capital of Kush was founded at Napata, on a bend of the Nile. The kingdom grew rich on the gold it traded with Egypt. After Napata was attacked, the capital was moved to Meroe on the other bank of the Nile.

Q What happened to Kush?

A Kush was a great kingdom for a thousand years. There is evidence of iron production and a high level of trading along the Nile. There were also great palaces and a temple to the Egyptian god, Amon. However, the Kush were overthrown by their neighbor, Aksum, around 300 A.D.

Q How did the kingdom of Aksum grow?

A Aksum was probably founded by a mixture of African and southern Arabian peoples. The capital, also called Aksum, was in the highlands, and there was an important port, called Adulis, which was a major trading point. From 300 B.C. to A.D. 600. Aksum grew rich on the ivory trade.

Q What can be seen of Aksum today?

A Aksum lies in what is now Ethiopia. The ruins of Aksum include a palace with twenty-seven carved thrones. There are also 126 granite columns, some over 98 feet high. Other columns are carved with pictures of multistory houses.

Q Did the Ancient Africans use iron?

A People living around Nok in Nigeria were making iron tools and weapons by about 5000 B.C. By A.D. 400 the use of iron had spread all the way down to southern Africa.

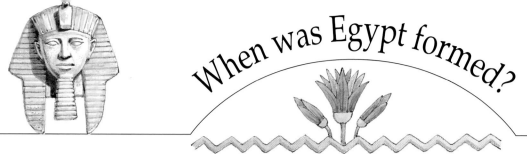

When was Egypt formed?

Pharaoh Ramesses II reigned for sixty-seven years and had over one hundred children.

Lower Egypt, the area around the Nile delta, and Upper Egypt were united under one ruler around 3100 B.C. The Egyptian civilization lasted until 30 B.C., when Egypt became part of the Roman Empire.

Q Why was the ruler called pharaoh?

A The Egyptians thought that their ruler was descended from the Sun god and it would not be respectful for an ordinary person to use his name. They referred to him as pharaoh, or "per a' o" as the Egyptians called him, which means "The Great House."

Q What did the Egyptians call their country?

A The Egyptians called their country "Kmt," which means "The Black Land." This refers to the rich soil along the riverbanks. The desert on either side of the Nile which protected Egypt from invasion by enemies and provided gold and gem stones was called "Dsrt," which means "The Red Land."

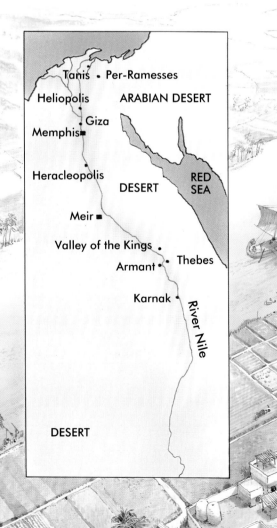

Tanis • Per-Ramesses
Heliopolis   ARABIAN DESERT
Memphis • Giza
Heracleopolis
DESERT   RED SEA
Meir ■
Valley of the Kings •
Armant • • Thebes
Karnak •
River Nile
DESERT

Q Where was the capital?

A The site of the capital changed at different times. The first was at Memphis, midway between Upper and Lower Egypt. During the Middle Kingdom the capital city was further south at Itj-towy. The New Kingdom pharaohs made Thebes the capital and a great religious center. The later capitals of Per-Ramesses and Tanis were in the Nile delta.

The Egyptians were the first people to have bathrooms.

The Egyptians made sticky bandages out of linen coated with honey.

Q When was Egyptian civilization at its height?

A Egypt was at its greatest during periods which historians call the Old Kingdom (2575-2134 B.C.), the Middle Kingdom (2040-1640 B.C.) and the New Kingdom (1552-1070 B.C.). Between these times the country was torn by civil war and after the New Kingdom it was invaded by Assyrians, Persians and Greeks.

Q Was the River Nile important?

A Not only did the River Nile give the Egyptians fish and duck to eat, its annual flooding left a rich layer of silt on its banks which made the soil fertile again. Papyrus reeds grew in the river. These could be made into baskets, mats, brushes and paper. The river also made trade possible as it could be used to transport goods, even heavy objects such as stone. Around ninety percent of Egyptians lived within 6 mi. of the Nile or its marshy delta.

Q Did they conquer other kingdoms?

A During the New Kingdom the pharoahs built up a powerful army of infantry and charioteers. They built an empire which stretched from Syria in the north to Sudan in the south.

Q Did Egypt trade with other countries?

A Egypt traded gold in return for cedar wood from Lebanon, and oil, wine and silver from lands further afield. Ebony, ivory and incense came from countries south of Egypt.

What was life like in Egypt?

Egyptian mothers gave their children beer to take to school for their lunch.

Historians have a good idea what life was like in Egypt thanks to documents written on papyrus, inscriptions on stone and wall paintings and objects found in tombs.

Q What did people wear?

A Due to the hot climate, people needed only light clothes, usually made of linen. Often clothes were not worn indoors. Slaves, laborers and children usually went naked. However, people cared very much about their appearance and keeping clean. Both men and women wore eye makeup, jewelery and perfume.

Q How did they amuse themselves?

A Wall paintings show women dancing and having picnics, and men wrestling and hunting duck, antelopes and hares. Board games were popular with adults as well as children, and many families kept pets.

Q What were their houses like?

A Homes, and even royal palaces, were made from sun-dried mud bricks. Stone was only used for tombs and temples. The hot weather and bright light meant that windows were small and placed high in the wall. Doors and windows often had screens made of matting to keep out flies and dust. In the hottest weather people slept on the flat roof.

Q Did people eat well?

A The Nile provided fish, eels, ducks and geese. Fruit, vegetables and pork were also important parts of the daily diet. The Egyptians introduced the watermelon from southern Africa and the fig from Turkey. They also knew how to make wine, beer and cheese. Wheat was used to make pastry and biscuits, often flavored with honey and herbs, and forty different kinds of bread.

Egyptian gods. From left to right: Hathor, Toth, Anubis, Osiris and Isis.

Q Was religion important?

A The fact that the Egyptians built so many huge temples shows that religion was very important to them. They worshipped many different gods and believed that there was life after death. This belief led them to preserve the bodies of the dead as mummies, and to bury them with food, tools and weapons for the afterlife. Priests were very powerful. Ordinary people believed they could tell the future from dreams and the stars, and even protect them from evil with charms and spells.

Q What work did people do?

A Most people were farmers. When there was no work in the fields they had time to help with the building of temples or pyramids. This was also a way of paying taxes. Skilled craftsmen were well paid, but they were paid in food, linen, firewood or salt, rather than money. Most women looked after their families, but they could also be weavers, dancers, nannies, priestesses, or makers of perfume and makeup.

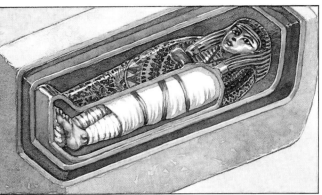

Q How were bodies made into mummies?

A The body was cut open and the heart, lungs and other organs were taken out and kept separately in a set of jars. The brain was pulled out through the nose with a hook, bit by bit, and thrown away. The body was then filled with natron, a natural salt which dried it out and stopped it from rotting. It was then stuffed with cloths and rolled in bandages before being buried inside two or three coffins. The whole business took about seventy days.

Q When did people work?

A People worked for eight days at a time and then had two days rest. There were also 65 holy days set aside for ceremonies and festivals. People also took time off for funerals and birthdays. Most work was done in two shifts during the cooler times of the day - morning and evening. People took a nap during the heat of midday.

The pyramids at Giza once had smooth sides but the outer stones have been removed, leaving the step shape we see today.

What can be seen of Ancient Egypt?

Egypt's dry desert air has preserved many of its ancient treasures. Modern Egypt's tourist industry is based on taking visitors to famous sites and museums.

Q Why were the pyramids built?

A Pyramids were built to guard the bodies of dead pharaohs and their treasures. The first pyramids were built before the Old Kingdom and had sides rising in steps. The pyramids at Giza were built during the Old Kingdom, and are the only one of the Seven Wonders of the Ancient World which can be seen today.

Q Which was the biggest pyramid?

A The pyramid built for Khufu is 755.9 ft. along each side and was originally 469 ft. high. Its four sides face exactly north, south, east and west. Around 2,300,000 blocks of stone were needed to build it, each one averaging over two tons and the largest weighing 17 tons. It took 100,000 men over twenty years to build it.

Q Who was Tutankhamun?

A Tutankhamun became pharaoh when he was nine years old and died at the age of nineteen in 1352 B.C. His tomb was discovered in 1922. Unlike almost all the other royal tombs it had not been robbed and was filled with wonderful treasures.

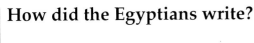

Here are the Karnak Ruins, which were once the royal treasury, form the largest group of ancient buildings in the world.

Q How did the Egyptians write?

A The Egyptians wrote in hieroglyphs, which were pictures of objects but could also be used to represent sounds. There were over 700 hieroglyphs.

Q What is the Rosetta Stone?

A The Rosetta Stone is a carved stone tablet with an inscription in Greek and hieroglyphic writing. It helped experts to understand hieroglyphics.

Q Is the Nile still important?

A The Nile is still vital to Egypt. Over ninety percent of the people still live along its banks or in its delta. The annual flood is now controlled by the High Dam at Aswan. This allows the water to be used more efficiently and some has been diverted for farming. The dam also generates electricity for industry.

Q What are the main sites that visitors can see?

A Near the ruins of Thebes are the temples of Luxor and Karnak, linked by an avenue of sphinxes 1.8 mi. long. On the south side of the Nile lies the "Valley of the Kings," where Tutankhamun's tomb was found. At Abu Simbel, near the border with Sudan, two massive temples in honor of Ramesses II were cut out of a sandstone cliff.

Greek merchants traded all over the Aegean, Mediterranean and Black Seas.

Who were the Greeks?

They set up many important colonies where they traded.

The Greeks lived in separate city states, scattered from southern Russia to Spain. Greek civilization flourished between 800 B.C. and 500 B.C. By 30 B.C. the Romans had taken over the Greek Empire.

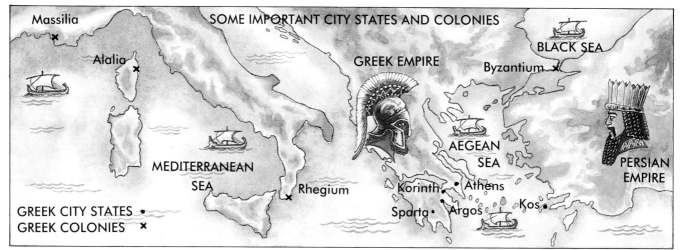

SOME IMPORTANT CITY STATES AND COLONIES

Massilia

Alalia

BLACK SEA

GREEK EMPIRE

Byzantium

MEDITERRANEAN SEA

AEGEAN SEA

PERSIAN EMPIRE

Rhegium

Korinth · Athens

Sparta · Argos

Kos

GREEK CITY STATES ·
GREEK COLONIES ×

Q What was a city state?

A Each city state consisted of a city and the land surrounding it. They had their own government, army and money system. Most of them were situated near the sea and traded with each other.

Q Which were the most important city states?

A The leading city state was Athens. Athens had rich silver mines, a big navy and factories making things such as weapons, furniture, pottery and leather goods. The main rival to Athens was Sparta. Sparta was a warlike city state where every citizen served in the army.

Q How big was Athens?

A Athens had a territory of about 617 sq. mi. and a population of around 200,000. Only about 40,000 of these were free men, who fought in the army and took part in government. The rest were women, children, slaves and foreigners, all of whom had fewer rights than the Athenian men.

Q How did the Greeks fight?

A The main strength of the Greek armies was the infantry. Soldiers wore a helmet, leg guards called greaves, and a bronze breastplate. They were armed with a sword and a 21 foot spear called a sarissa. They also carried a large round shield. These soldiers were organized into disciplined groups called phalanxes. The Greeks also had a cavalry and a navy.

Q Who was Alexander the Great?

A Alexander was the King of Macedonia. He built a huge empire, stretching from Greece to the borders of India. He founded many cities, and spread the Greek culture through the Middle East. Alexander died in 323 B.C. at the age of 33.

Q Who were the Greek's main enemies?

A The powerful Persian Empire was the main threat to the Greeks. Between 490 B.C. and 479 B.C. the Greeks united to defeat two large Persian invasions. Sometimes the different city states fought each other. Athens and Sparta had a long war with each other, from 431 B.C. to 404 B.C., which Sparta eventually won.

Q What were Greek warships like?

A The most powerful warship was the trireme, which had three rows of oars, rowed by 170 men. It used sails when possible, but used its oars during calm weather or when it was going to ram another ship with its 9.8 ft. ram. It could travel at up to 9 mph.

How did the Greeks live?

Lots of writers used to live in Athens, so much is known about the way people lived at this time.

Q Did people eat well?

A Greek food was plain but healthy - fish, barley bread, goat's cheese, olives, figs, fruit, vegetables and salads flavored with parsley or basil. Meat was only eaten at festivals. Poor people ate lupins, a kind of flower, and grasshoppers.

Q What did Greeks learn at school?

A Apart from teaching how to read and write, schools also taught poetry, music and physical education. The Greeks thought that the ideal man should be able to fight, make speeches and entertain his friends. Girls did not go to school but learned how to spin and weave from their mothers.

Q How did people travel?

A Donkeys were used to carry people and goods short distances. As Greece is so mountainous it was usually easier to travel longer distances by boat around the coast rather than go overland.

Q How did women live?

A Women in Athens played little part in public life, except at religious festivals. They got married at age 13 or 14 and spent most of their time at home. They were allowed to own clothes, jewels and slaves; but not land or houses. Women in Sparta were treated equally to men and could own land, but they did not fight in the army.

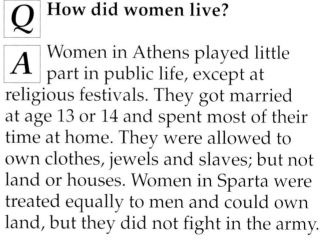

Q What sort of religion did the Greeks have?

A The Greeks worshipped many gods and their greatest buildings were temples put up in honor of the gods. Only priests were allowed inside the temples. Sacrifices and other ceremonies were held outside.

Q What did people wear?

A The main item of clothing that men and women wore was the tunic. They also wore woolen cloaks, straw hats and leather sandals. Rich Greeks could afford silk clothes and expensive dyes to color their clothes, but most people wore lightweight linen and woolen clothes. Brooches and pins were used to hold clothes in place as buttons were not used.

Q What gods did they worship?

A The Greeks believed that the gods lived on Mount Olympus, the highest mountain in Greece. The most powerful god was Zeus, king of the gods. There were gods or goddesses for every aspect of life, such as war, love, music and hunting.

Zeus

Athena

Hera

Hermes

Only men were allowed to act in Greek plays. All actors wore masks.

Greek culture has had a lasting effect on later European history, in both the arts and sciences.

Q Did the Greeks make any scientific discoveries?

A The Greeks developed the scientific ideas that they discovered in Babylon and Egypt. For example, they knew that the Earth traveled around the Sun. They also invented steam engines. The ideas of Pythagoras and Euclid are still taught today.

Q What was the importance of Greek art and architecture?

A The Greek style of building was copied by the Romans and has been used by architects ever since, especially for public buildings, such as museums and town halls. Greek buildings were often decorated with bronze or marble statues. Many of these statues can be seen in museums all around the world.

Q Did the Greeks have myths and legends?

A The Greeks had many stories about heroes, such as Herakles (Hercules). There are also many stories about monsters, like the bull-headed Minotaur, the one-eyed Cyclops and the Gorgon, called Medusa, who could turn people to stone. These stories have been retold ever since Greek times.

The Greeks dated their history from 776 B.C., when the first Olympics were held.

Q How did the Greeks cure their sick?

A The Greeks were one of the first peoples to cure the sick using herbs, baths, exercise and diet rather than rely on so-called magic spells. Hippocrates of Kos (460-357 B.C.) is the most famous of all the Greek doctors. His ideas were still being studied 2,000 years after his death.

Q Did the Greeks go to the theater?

A The theater was very popular in Ancient Greece. The theater at Epidaurus could seat 14,000 people. "Drama," "theatre," "comedy," "chorus," "scenery," "tragedy" and "orchestra" are all originally Greek words. Many Greek plays by Athenian writers such as Sophokles are still put on today.

Q Did the Greeks play sports?

A The Greeks took sports very seriously. Running, wrestling and throwing the javelin were good training for war. Festivals, called games, were held every four years at four separate sites around Greece. The games at Olympia were the most important. The competitions included poetry and music as well as athletics. Only men were allowed into the games The modern Olympics were based on these games and were first held in Athens in 1896.

The cavalry in the Roman army was usually made up of non-Romans. They were called auxiliaries.

How big was the Roman Empire?

The Roman Empire covered all of the Mediterranean, much of Europe and even north Africa. It began around 753 B.C. and lasted over one thousand years.

 Q Who founded Rome?

A According to Roman legend the twins Romulus and Remus founded Rome. As babies they were left to die, but were saved and cared for by wolves. The legend says they founded Rome in 753 B.C., with Romulus naming the city after himself and becoming the first king. However, historians think that the first kings were probably Etruscans who founded the city on the seven hills by the Tiber River in the seventh century B.C.

Q Who were the Etruscans?

A Very little is known about the Etruscans as their language is still not properly understood. Originally, they came from Turkey, and were at their height of power around 550 B.C. They were an advanced civilization which, amongst other things, wore robes like Roman togas and built the first drains in Rome.

Q How did Rome grow?

A At first Rome was only a weak city state. The Romans built a wall around the seven hills to defend themselves and built up a strong army. By 264 B.C. they had conquered all of Italy.

Britain
Germany
France
THE ROMAN EMPIRE
Spain
Italy
Rome
Africa

Q What were the Punic Wars?

A Rome's expansion brought it into conflict with the empire of Carthage (see page 12). Between 264 B.C. and 146 B.C. Rome fought three long wars with Carthage ending in total victory for Rome. In the course of these wars Rome conquered Sicily, Sardinia, Corsica, Spain and southern France.

All Roman roads had milestones which measured the distance from the city of Rome.

Q Why was the Roman army important?

A The army conquered Rome's empire and defended it against its enemies. The main strength of the army was the infantry who often won against much larger numbers because they were so well armed, trained and disciplined. They were also good at building fortifications and besieging cities.

Q Why were Roman roads important?

A The Romans built excellent roads which allowed their soldiers to move quickly between forts and boundaries. Merchants also used the roads, so trade flourished. There were over 52,800 mi. of roads which were so well built that they lasted for centuries.

Julius Caesar

Q Who was Julius Caesar?

A Julius Caesar was a famous general who conquered most of France. He was also a good public speaker and was popular with Romans. He made himself ruler of Rome, but was murdered by former friends who thought that Rome should be a republic and not ruled by one man.

Julius Caesar changed the calendar from 355 days a year to the 365-day system we use now.

What was life like in Rome?

A million people lived in Rome in A.D. 200. However, not everyone was well off. By A.D. 270, around 300,000 people were unemployed and lived on free handouts of barley bread, pork fat and olive oil from the government.

Q What did people eat?

A Rich Romans ate ham from Gaul or oysters from Britannia and spiced their food with pepper from India or ginger from China. Rice, sugar and carrots were known of but rarely eaten. Sheep and goat's milk was preferred to cow's milk. Poor people ate bean soup.

Q What were their homes like?

A Poor people lived in badly-built apartment blocks without bathrooms or kitchens. They used public baths and got hot food from cook-shops. The houses of rich Romans faced inwards on to an open space, called an atrium, with arcades to provide shade from the hot sun. Rich people often had big villas and estates in the country.

Q How did people keep clean and healthy?

A All Roman cities had public baths, like modern leisure centers, where people could bathe and swim. Romans also visited the baths to work out at the gymnasium, watch acrobats, gamble or chat with friends and buy snacks.

The Romans introduced football to Britain in A.D. 200.

Q Who did all the work?

A Nearly one third of the population were slaves, who did all the work. If they were educated they might have a comfortable life as a tutor, book keeper, doctor, or musician with a wealthy family. However, farmers, laborers and miners had a hard life and usually a short one.

Q What entertainments were there?

A As slaves did most of the work, many Roman citizens had time for leisure. Like the Greeks, they enjoyed the theater. The word "pantomime" comes from the Roman word for a mimed show. Even more popular were games which included chariot racing and combats in which gladiators fought each other or wild beasts.

Q What did the Romans believe in?

A The Romans adopted many Greek gods. They called Zeus "Jupiter," Poseidon "Neptune," Hermes "Mercury," and Aphrodite "Venus." Emperors were worshipped as gods after their death. When they came to live in a colony such as Britain, they often added in local gods as well. Romans also believed in household spirits, and in fortune telling through astrology, dice, palm reading, sacrifices and interpreting natural events, like lightning or flocks of birds.

Q How were people punished?

A The Romans had a very complicated system of law. Punishments for law breaking or minor offences, included fines or whipping. Major crimes might lead to loss of citizenship, banishment to a distant place or being sent to work in a mine or as a galley slave. Execution might be by beheading, drowning, crucifixion or being made to fight in the games. Prisons were only used to detain people until they were punished in some other way.

The word "pen" comes from the Latin for feather.

What was the impact of Roman rule?

Roman rule had its greatest impact in northwest Europe, where Romans built the first cities and roads. Roman rule had less impact in Greece, Egypt and the Middle East where there were already long established civilizations.

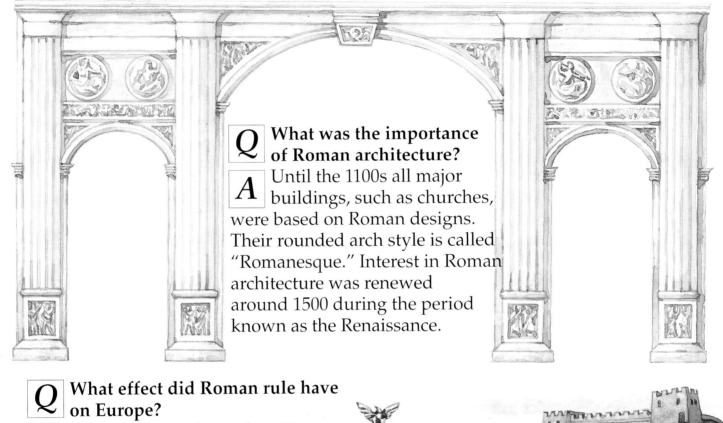

Q What was the importance of Roman architecture?

A Until the 1100s all major buildings, such as churches, were based on Roman designs. Their rounded arch style is called "Romanesque." Interest in Roman architecture was renewed around 1500 during the period known as the Renaissance.

Q What effect did Roman rule have on Europe?

A Many of the main roads in Europe still follow the lines of old Roman roads. Also, many place names are linked to their Roman past. For example place names in England ending in -caster or -chester come from "castra," the Latin word for a military camp or fort.

Only the Roman emperor and his family were allowed to wear purple cloth.

Q How did Roman rule affect Christianity?

A Roman emperors often persecuted Christians because they refused to worship them as gods. However the emperor, Constantine, had a Christian mother, and Christianity then became the official religion of the empire.

Q Why was Latin important?

A After Roman rule had ended Latin was used as the written language of learning, government and religion throughout most of Europe for a thousand years. Over the same period Latin as a spoken language developed into Italian, French, Spanish, Portugese and Romanian. English, which developed from German, has thousands of words from Latin.

Q How has Roman history inspired art and literature?

A Roman history has inspired artists and historians for centuries. Shakespeare wrote the plays *Julius Ceasar* and *Antony and Cleopatra* a thousand years after the Romans left Britain. More recently the nineteenth century novels *Quo Vadis* and *The Last Days of Pompeii* have been made into films.

Q Where can Roman remains be seen today?

A Impressive ruins can be seen in most of the countries around the Mediterranean Sea. The Colosseum and Pantheon are two of the most impressive ruins in Rome. Pompeii, a Roman town, was preserved under a layer of volcanic ash when Mount Vesuvius erupted in A.D. 79. There are also many important remains in Britain such as Hadrian's Wall and Fishbourne Villa.

Index